B

WHEELS

MAKE IT MOVE

Wendy Arnold-Dean

Photographs by Chris Fairclough

Belitha Press

First published in Great Britain in 1993 by
🟢 Belitha Press Limited
31 Newington Green, London N16 9PU

Copyright © Belitha Press Ltd 1993

All rights reserved.
No part of this book may be reproduced or utilized
in any form or by any means, electronic or mechanical,
including photocopying, recording or by any information storage
and retrieval system, without permission in writing from the Publisher.
Printed in China for Imago

ISBN 1 85561 200 3

British Library Cataloguing in Publication Data CIP data
for this book is available from the British Library

Acknowledgements
Thank you to our models: Imogen, Jack, Murriam, Nathaniel and Oliver,
also to Jem Racing and Jeremy for the kart shots.
Editor: Rachel Cooke
Designers: Howland Northover
Toys: Deborah Crow
Artwork: David Gifford

To Joe Arun

CONTENTS

What is a wheel? 4
Why are wheels so useful? 6
Bits and pieces 10
1: Wheels 12
2: Axles 14
3: The body 16
Wheels for transport 18
4: The head 20
5: Up and down 22
6: Off we go 24
Making wheels move 26
Variations 28
Wheels all around us 30
Glossary and index 32

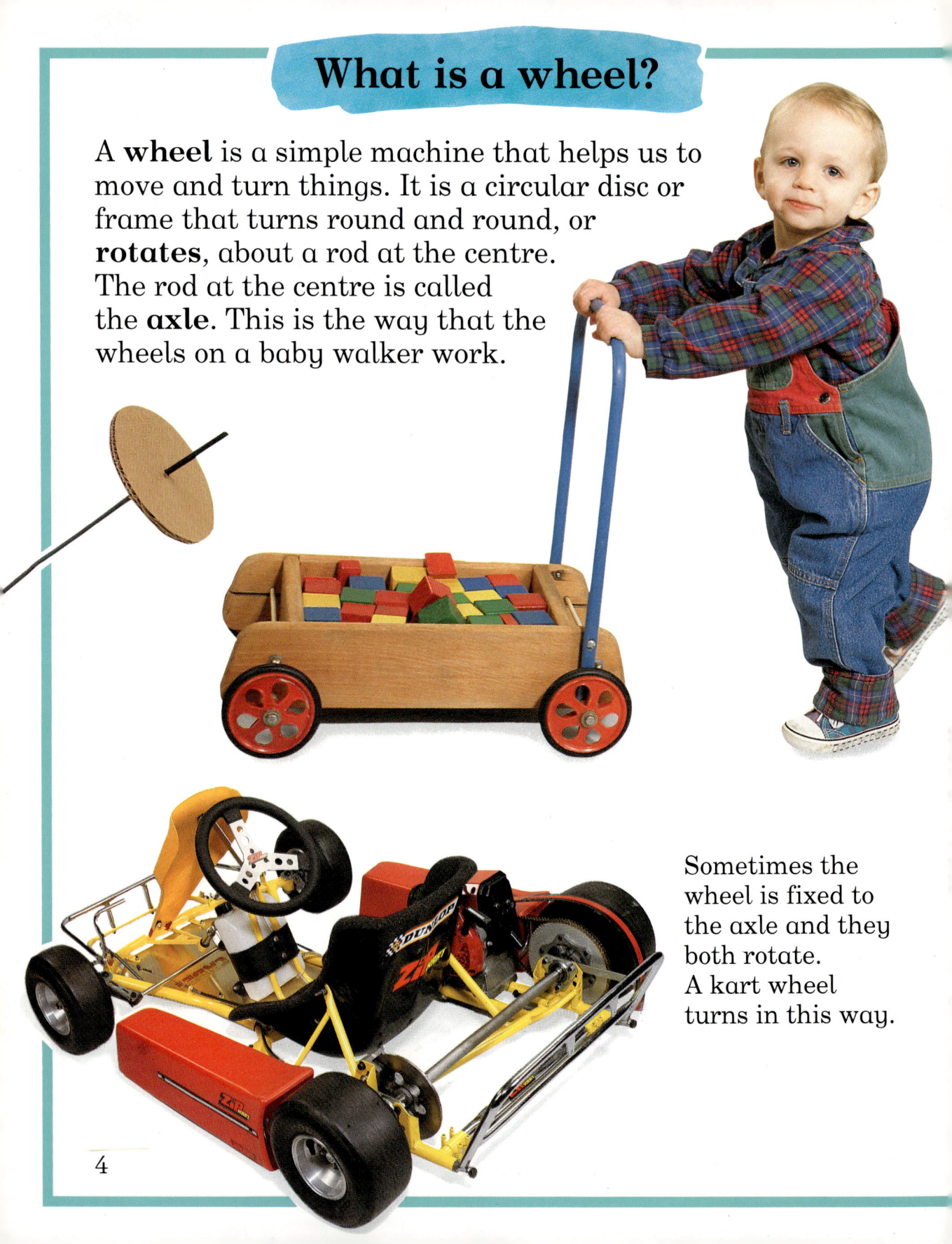

What is a wheel?

A **wheel** is a simple machine that helps us to move and turn things. It is a circular disc or frame that turns round and round, or **rotates**, about a rod at the centre. The rod at the centre is called the **axle**. This is the way that the wheels on a baby walker work.

Sometimes the wheel is fixed to the axle and they both rotate. A kart wheel turns in this way.

Wheels are all around us. Wheels help us to do so many different things that it is hard to imagine what the world would be like without them. This book shows you many of the ways we use wheels in our everyday lives.

You can also find out for yourself just how wheels work, by making your own push along tortoise toy. It rolls its eyes and nods its head. You move it by using wheels.

Why are wheels so useful?

Wheels can help us to move heavy objects more easily.

Before the wheel was invented, people had to move heavy objects by dragging them on the ground.

To make things easier they used large round poles or tree trunks placed underneath the object as rollers.

This was still hard work because someone had to keep moving the rollers to the front.

The wheel made things so much easier that many people say it is one of the most important of all inventions.

Wheels can be used in this way to move things and people.

You can turn wheels to help you control something.

A steering wheel turns the wheels on a car, and a record player turns a record.

Some wheels are designed specially to do a particular job. This wheel is used for cutting.

These wheels are made wide and flat for pressing and rolling.

Pulleys and **gear-wheels** are special kinds of wheels that have been changed to do specific jobs. Can you see how they have been changed?

9

Bits and pieces

The things on these pages are the ones you will need to make your push along tortoise toy. You will find the shapes drawn full size at the front of the book. Trace them onto thin paper and cut the shapes out. You can use these paper shapes to draw round on the card you use to make your toy.

If you don't want to use these shapes, you can always make up your own.

10

You will need

thin paper
a pencil
scissors
corrugated card
glue
3 thin sticks –
  dowel, garden
  or barbecue
sticky tape
strong card
a paper fastener
a cork
coloured pens
  and paper for
  decoration

1 Wheels

To start your tortoise toy, you first need to make the wheels.

1

Trace around shape A at the front of the book, using some thin paper and mark the centre. Cut it out. This is your template for the wheels.

2

Put the template for shape A on the corrugated card. Draw around it 8 times. Remember to mark the centre on each piece.

3

Cut out the 8 circles.

4

Glue 2 circles together to make a thick wheel. Repeat this with the other circles to make 4 wheels in all. Make sure that you can still see the centre mark on each side.

Circles and wheels

Circles can be hard to draw and make. People often use a pair of compasses to help them to draw or cut exact circles. You might like to try using some of these when you make the wheels of your toy.

For wheels to turn around smoothly it is important that the circles are exactly round. The axle should be in the centre. How do you think the wheels would move if this was not so?

2 Axles

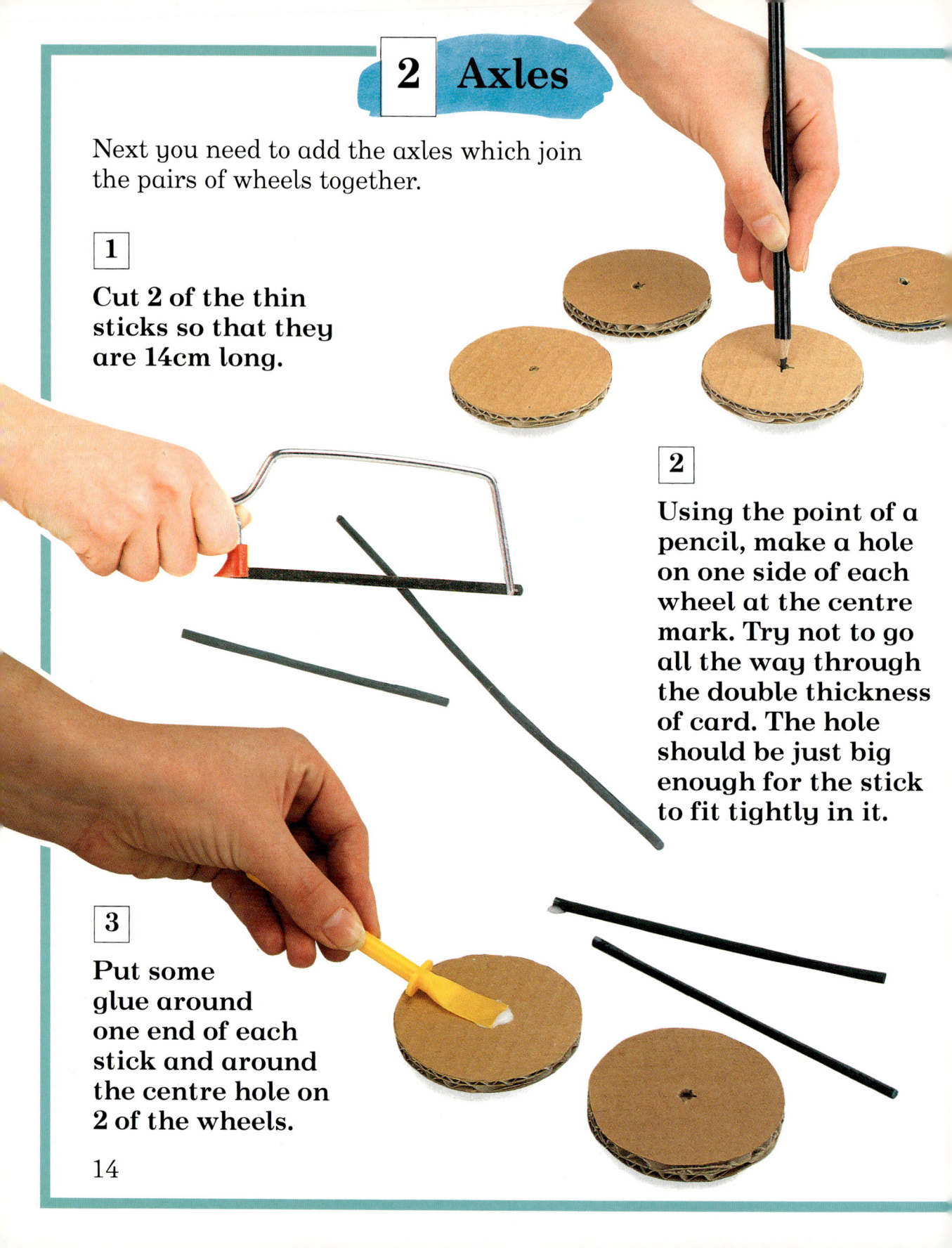

Next you need to add the axles which join the pairs of wheels together.

1

Cut 2 of the thin sticks so that they are 14cm long.

2

Using the point of a pencil, make a hole on one side of each wheel at the centre mark. Try not to go all the way through the double thickness of card. The hole should be just big enough for the stick to fit tightly in it.

3

Put some glue around one end of each stick and around the centre hole on 2 of the wheels.

4

Push one wheel onto the end of each stick carefully. Make sure that the wheel is tight and straight. Leave for a while to let the glue dry. The other wheels will be added later.

Axles and wheels

The **axle** is a rod or pin around which the wheel turns, or **rotates**. Wheels are often joined in pairs by an axle. Some wheels rotate around the axle which is fixed to a frame. This is how this hamster wheel works.

Some wheels are fixed to the axle, which means that the axle and wheels rotate together. Your tortoise toy will have this type of wheel. Turn one of the axles you have just attached to a wheel. When it turns so does the wheel.

3 The body

The wheels on the toy must be attached to a frame to keep them steady. This will be the body of the tortoise.

1

Make a paper template of shape B at the front of the book. Use this to draw and cut out two semi-circle shapes from some stiff card. (You can use corrugated card again if you like.)

2

Using a template of shape C, cut out a long strip of the same stiff card. To make the body, join the two semi-circle shapes together with this strip, using sticky tape. The picture shows the best way to do this.

3

Make marks 4cm along and 1cm up from the bottom of each end of the body's two sides.

4

Cut holes at these 4 marks. Make the holes large enough for the axle sticks to fit through easily.

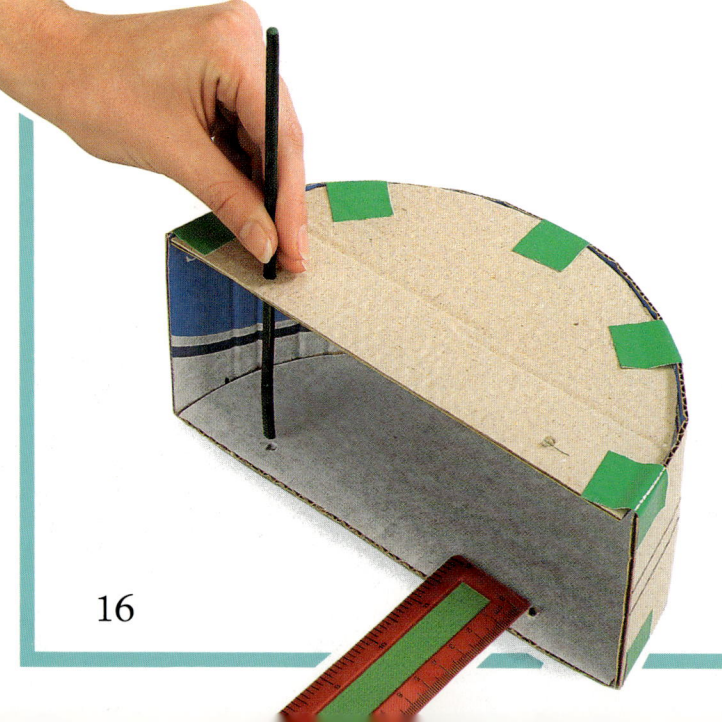

16

5

Push the 2 axles through the holes you have just made. Each axle should go through 2 opposite holes. The picture shows you how.

6

Glue the second 2 wheels onto the other ends of the axles in the same way as before.

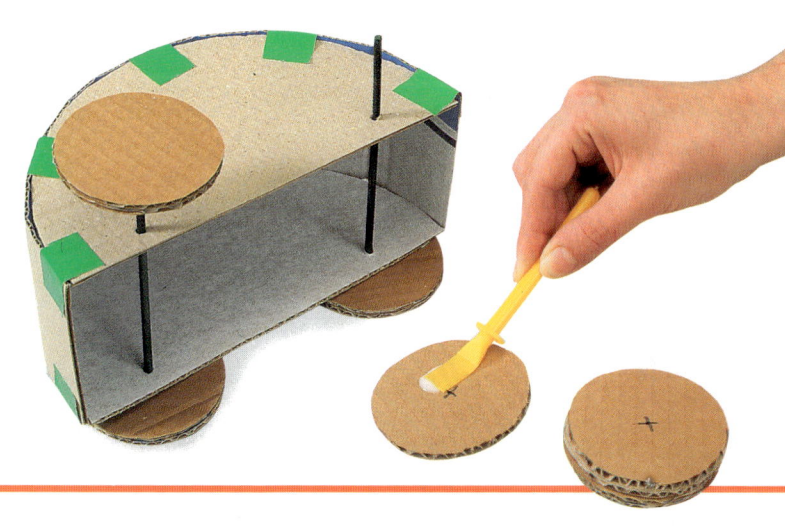

The chassis

The simple frame with the wheels and axles fixed to it is called the **chassis**. Most vehicles have a chassis. The rest of the vehicle, the body, is then built onto the chassis. It is important that the chassis is very strong.

Can you see the chassis in these vehicles?

Wheels for transport

Many of the types of transport we use today rely on wheels in some way.

Even aeroplanes use wheels to take off and land.

Wheels are usually placed in pairs, but not always. Many different numbers and combinations are used. Look at these pictures. How many different combinations can you see?

Gripping
Wheels for transport need to have a good grip on the ground. Otherwise they might skid or slide. Many wheels have a rough surface to help them grip.

18

Steering

Wheels often need to be turned or **steered**, to change the direction of the vehicle. Usually something is joined to the axle which can be used to turn it. The handle bars on a bicycle and the steering wheel on a car are used in this way.

Some wheels and axles can turn all the way around like on this shopping trolley.

How do you think you change direction on these wheels?

19

4 The head

Your tortoise has got a body and wheels for legs. Now it needs a head.

1

Draw 2 head shapes on the card, using a paper template of shape D. Mark the eye and paper fastener holes. Cut out the 2 head shapes and the eye holes.

2

Using a paper template of shape E, make the eye wheel. Mark the eye positions and paper fastener hole on both sides of the wheel. Draw and colour the eyes on both sides. You could make up some of your own eye shapes.

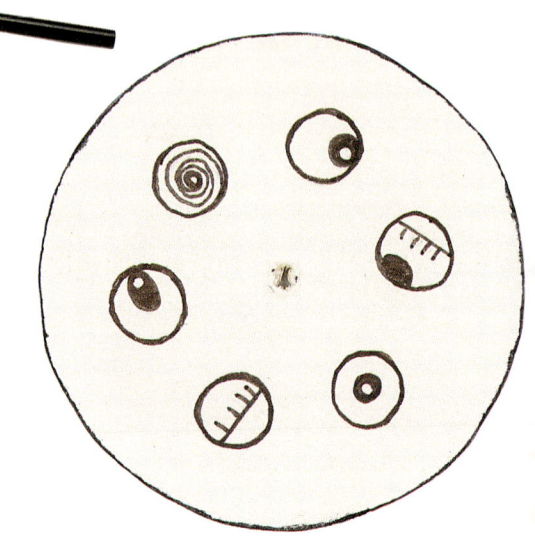

3

Join the eye wheel to 1 of the head shapes using a paper fastener through the marked points. Make sure that the eye wheel can be turned easily.

4

Cut the third stick so it is 26cm long. Tape the stick firmly to the neck part of the head shape.

5

Glue or tape the second head shape onto the back of the first. Take care not to glue over the moving parts.

The wheel you have just made is used to make the tortoise's eyes move and change. There are many other ways that wheels can be used to make pictures move or to create a special effect.

5 Up and down

The head is ready to be attached to the body.

1

Cut a slit half way along the front of the tortoise's body, about 6cm deep. This is shown on template C, so you may have already cut the slit out. It should be wide enough for the head stick to go through easily.

2

Punch a hole at the rear of the body above the axle line. Push the head stick through the slit and above the 2 axles, to the hole in the back of the body.

3

Tape the stick to the back of the body in the middle. The stick should lie just above the back axle without touching it.

4

Tape the cork firmly onto the front axle, in the middle. The head stick should lie directly over the cork on the axle.

Cams

A **cam** can be used to change the movement of a toy or machine from round and round (rotary) to up and down or backwards and forwards. Movement that is up and down or backwards and forwards in a line is called **linear**. You have made a cam on your toy using the cork. The wheels on the tortoise go round and round, which makes the axles and the cam turn too. The head stick rests on the cam and is made to bob up and down as the tortoise is pushed along. The head stick follows the movement of the cam and is called a **follower**. You have made a cam and follower.

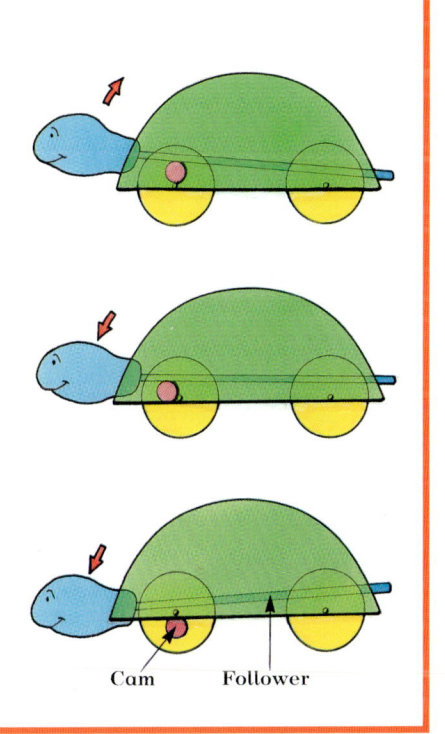

Cam   Follower

23

6 Off we go

Your toy can now be decorated to look more like a tortoise.

Your tortoise is ready to go. Make sure that the head stick is resting on the cork.
Turn the eyes wheel by moving the part sticking out under the tortoise's chin.
The eyes will move and change.

24

Put the tortoise on the ground and push it along. The head will bob up and down as it goes along.

Your tortoise can now go off nodding and looking wherever you want it to.

The wheels of your tortoise toy are moved by you pushing it along the ground. This is the **force** that moves it.

Here are some more wheels that are moved by being pushed.

25

Making wheels move

Wheels can be moved using different forces. They can be pulled as well as pushed.

The wind or water can be used.

They can be wound up.

Or they can be moved using a motor.

27

Variations

Why not try designing and making some different push along toys that move using wheels?

There are some ideas on these 2 pages.

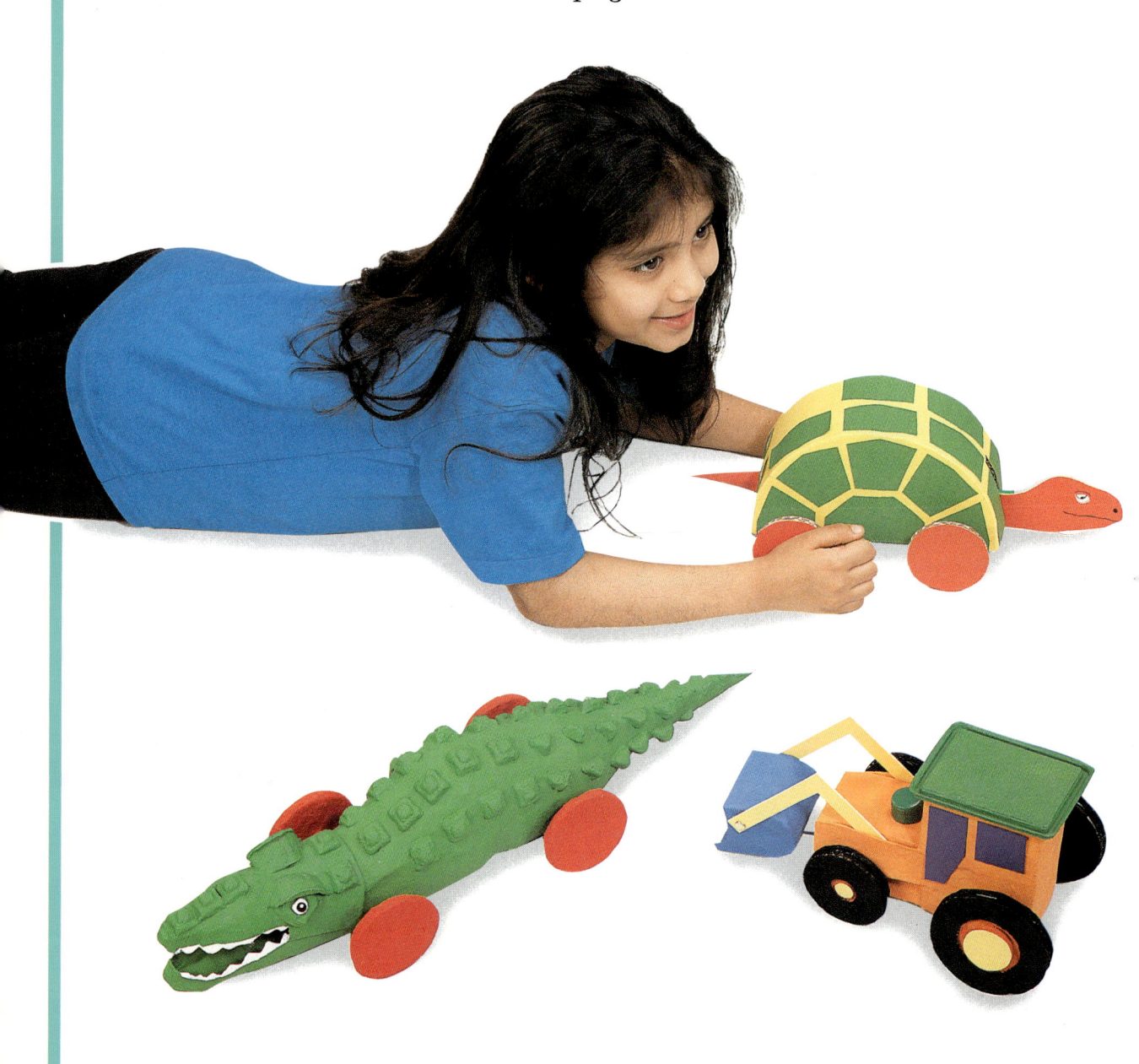

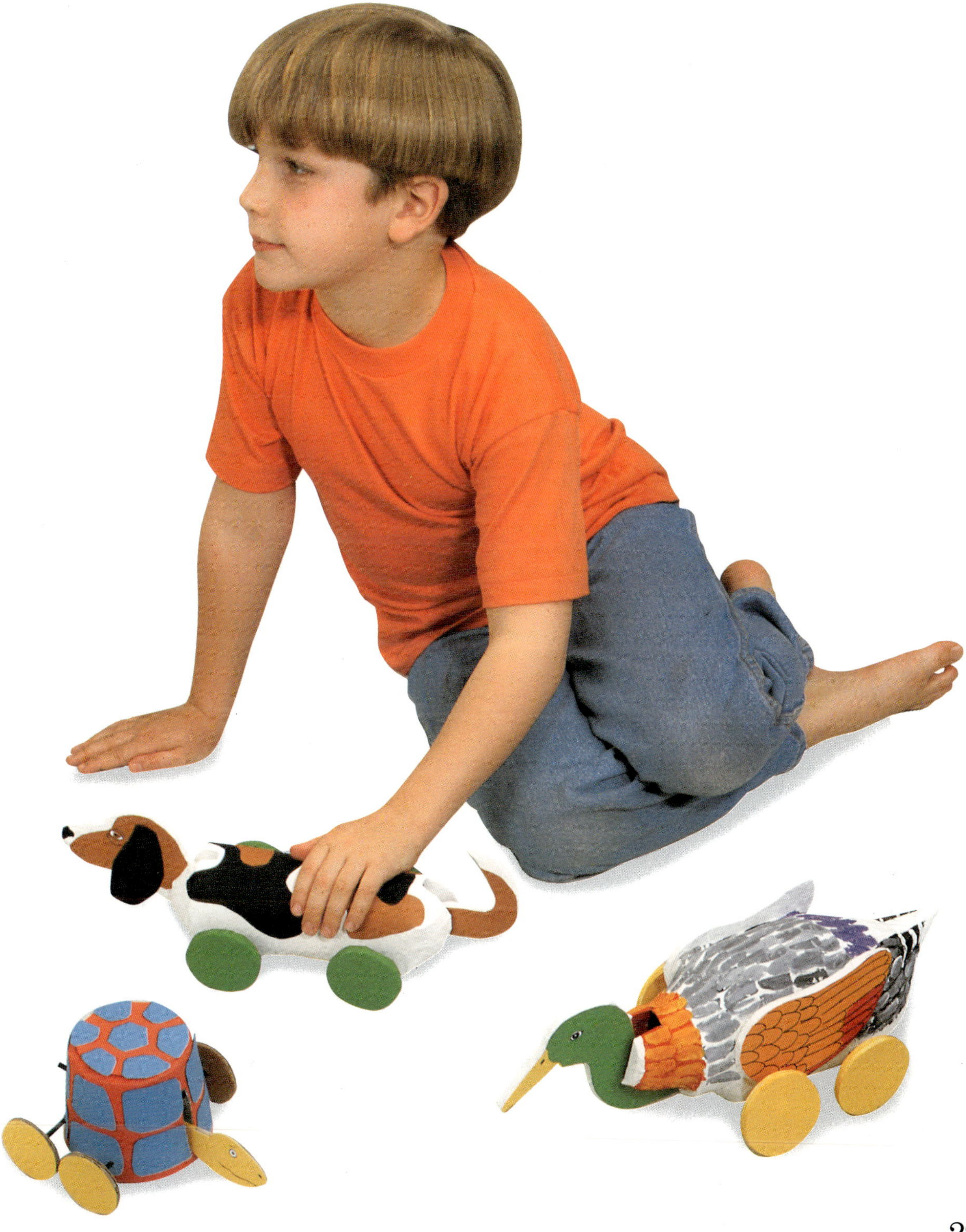

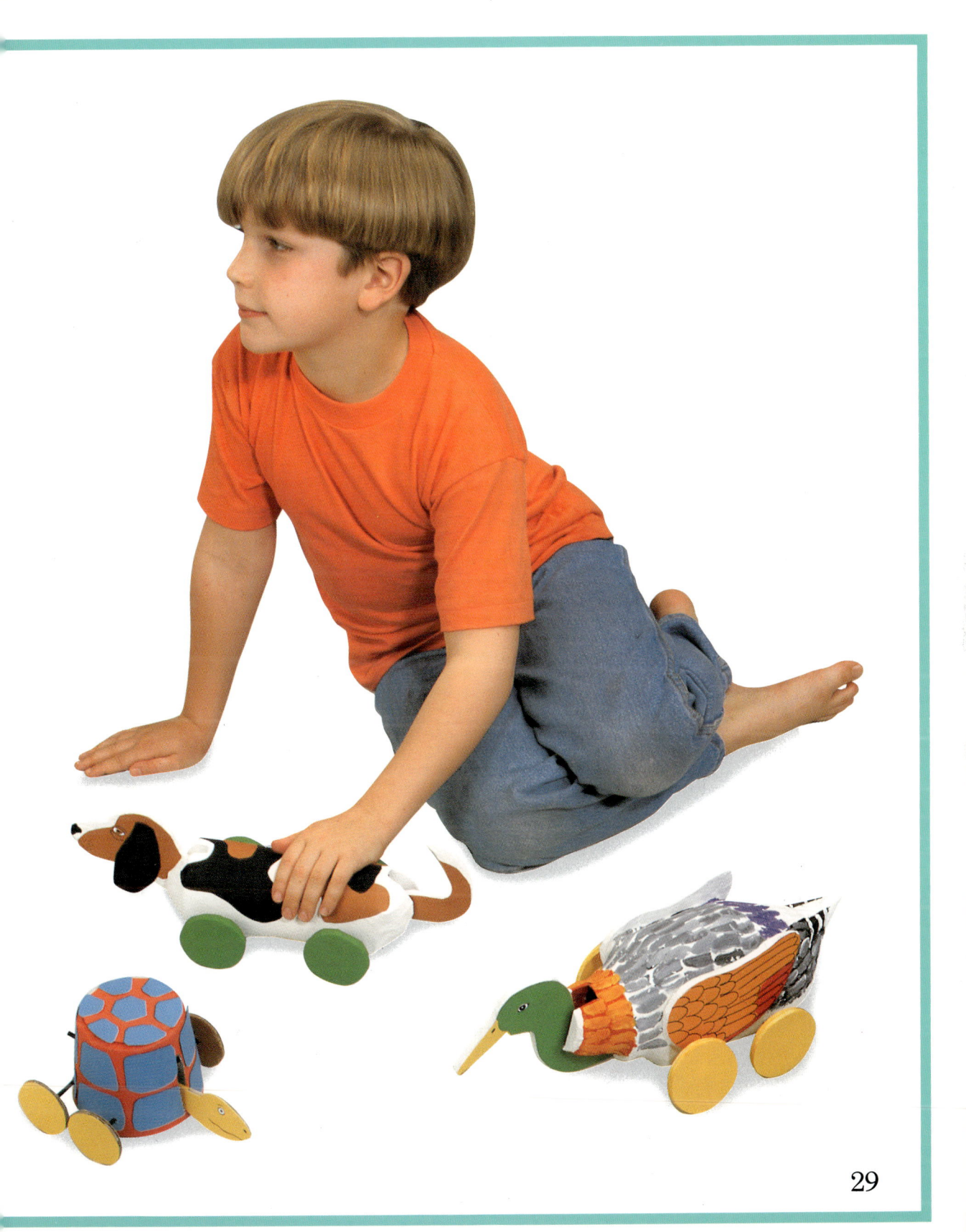

Wheels all around us

There are many types of toys and machines that use wheels. Here are just a few examples.

What other things can you think of that use wheels?
Look around you to see how many you can find.

31

Glossary

These are some useful words you may need when talking about wheels. They are shown in darker type when they first appear in the book or when they are explained.

Axle: the rod or pin to which a *wheel* is attached. The wheel turns on or around the axle.

Cam: a *wheel* with a projecting part, or an irregular shape, designed to change rotary movement (see *rotate*) to linear movement.

Chassis: the basic frame of a vehicle including the *wheels* and *axles*.

Follower: the part of a machine that is moved by the *cam*. The follower usually rests on the cam and is moved up and down as the cam turns around.

Force: the strength or power used to move something. *Wheels* need some kind of force to make them move.

Gear-wheel: a *wheel* with projections or teeth added to link with other gear-wheels or a chain. Many bicycles have gear-wheels.

Linear: something in the shape of a line. Linear movement is movement in a straight line.

Pulley: a *wheel* with a groove at the rim or a wide wheel, designed to take a rope or cord around it.

Rotate: to turn round and round about a fixed centre. A *wheel* rotates on or around its *axle*. This kind of movement is called rotary.

Steer: to direct or guide a moving object. Handle bars are used to steer a bicycle.

Wheel: a circular disc or frame that *rotates* on or about an *axle*. A wheel is a simple machine that helps us to move and turn things.

Index

axle 4, 13, 14-15, 17, 19, 23
cam 23
chassis 17
circles 13
follower 23
forces 25, 26-27
gear-wheels 9
linear movement 23

pulleys 9
toy tortoise, making 12-17, 19- 25
toy tortoise, variations 28-29
wheels, all around us 5
wheels for transport 18-19
wheels, movement 4, 13, 15, 26-27
wheels, special effects with 21
wheels, uses 5, 6-9, 18-19

C

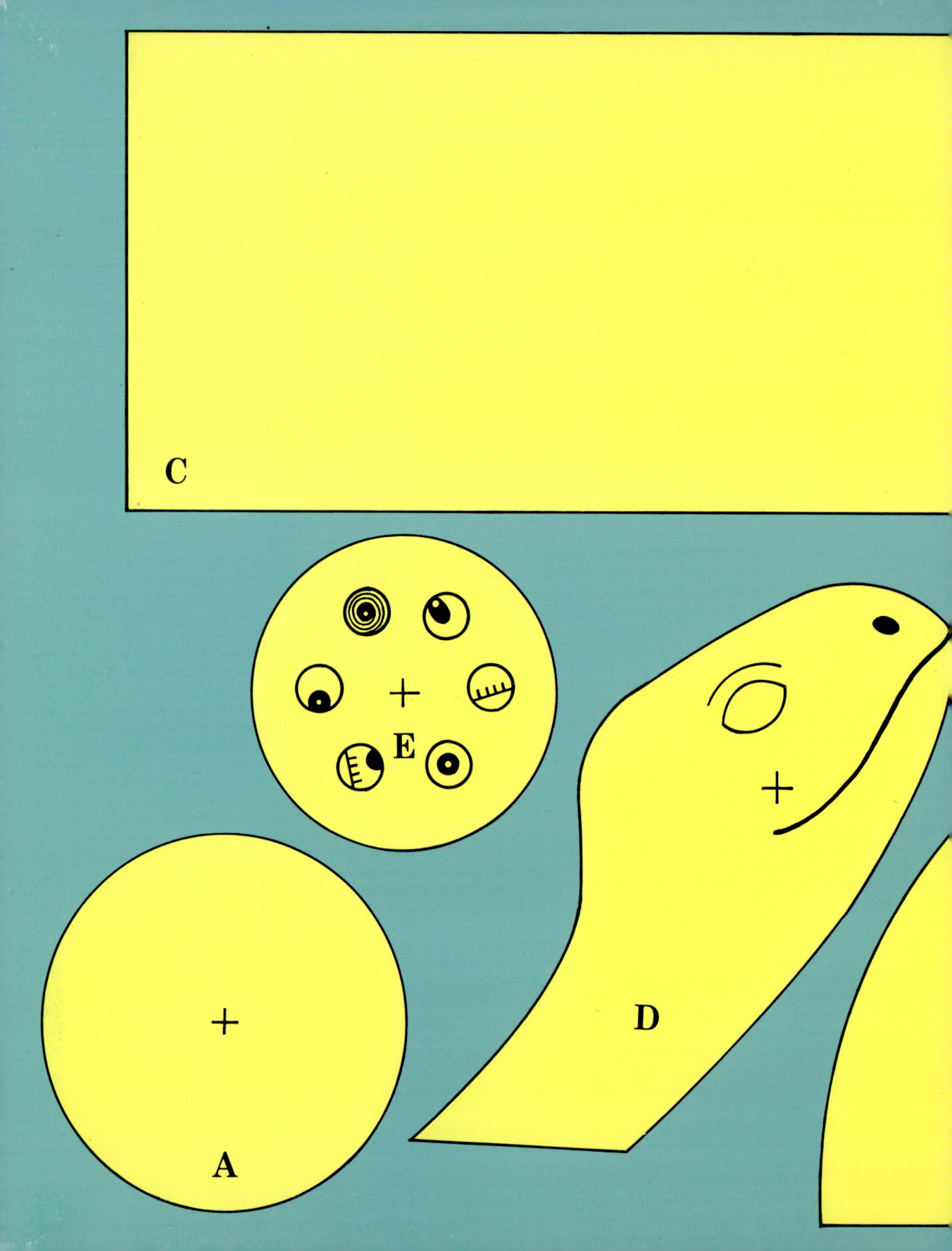

E

D

A